11/14

W9-AAW-726

Science to the Rescue

Swept Away by the Storm

Can science save your life?

Gerry Bailey

Crabtree Publishing Company
www.crabtreebooks.com

Crabtree Publishing Company
www.crabtreebooks.com
1-800-387-7650

PMB 59051, 350 Fifth Ave.
59th Floor,
New York, NY 10118

616 Welland Ave.
St. Catharines, ON
L2M 5V6

Published by Crabtree Publishing in 2014

Author: Gerry Bailey
Illustrator: Leighton Noyes
Editor: Shirley Duke
Proofreader: Crystal Sikkens
Production coordinator and
  Prepress technician: Tammy McGarr
Print coordinator: Margaret Amy Salter

Photographs:
All images are Shutterstock.com unless otherwise stated.
Pg 1 - Zacarias Pereira da Mata
Pg 2/3 - Zacarias Pereira da Mata
Pg 6 – Palo_ok   Pg 8/9 –tropicdreams
Pg 8 – (b)Claude Hoot
Pg 9 - (b) BMJ (m) feathercollector
Pg 10/11 – bikeriderlondon
Pg 12/13 – (t) NASA   Pg 12 – (b) paintings
Pg 13 – (b) MISHELLA   Pg 14/15 – DarkOne
Pg 16 – (t) BarryTuck (m) Frank L Junior
(b) Longjourneys   Pg 18 - NASA
Pg 18/19 - Nickolay Vinokurov
Pg 19 – Andrew Lever   Pg 20/21 - Nejron Photo
Pg 23 – (l) Anna segren
(r) Hannes Vos
Pg 24/25 – James BO Insogna   Pg 24 – fongfong
Pg 25 – (tl) Makushin Alexey (tm) Zorandim
(tr) wikipedia.org   Pg 26/27 – welcomia
Pg 26 – (b) Zacarias Pereira da Mata
Pg 27 – (b) Gail Johnson
Pg 29 - Wutthichai
Wave frieze – Noel Powell

Printed in Canada/032014/BF20140212

Library and Archives Canada Cataloguing in Publication

Bailey, Gerry, author
    Swept away by the storm / Gerry Bailey.

(Science to the rescue)
Includes index.
Issued in print and electronic formats.
ISBN 978-0-7787-0431-7 (bound).--ISBN 978-0-7787-0437-9 (pbk.).--
ISBN 978-1-4271-7543-4 (html).--ISBN 978-1-4271-7549-6 (pdf)

    1. Oceanography--Juvenile literature. I. Title.

GC21.5.B35 2014   j551.46   C2014-901062-1
                                          C2014-901063-X

Library of Congress Cataloging-in-Publication Data

CIP available at Library of Congress

Contents

Joe's story

Hi! I am a scientist named Joe, and I have a story to tell you—a real adventure!

I got stranded on a small boat out at sea. I hadn't gone far from shore and would have been okay, but a storm blew up very suddenly. It swept me into a fast-flowing current and out to sea.

I managed to survive with the help of all the science I knew.
But it's a long story.

Gather around and I'll tell you how it all happened.

I set out that morning in a small rowboat. I wasn't planning to go far from shore and I didn't have much equipment. The weather was fair and the sea was calm. I didn't intend to stay out for very long. Everything looked good.

What's an ocean?

An ocean is a huge body of salt water. Oceans cover nearly three-quarters of Earth's surface. The world's five oceans are connected and their waters flow in and out of each other. They are the Atlantic, Pacific, Arctic, Indian, and Southern oceans.

Arctic

Atlantic

Pacific

Southern

Currents and winds

Storms that mix up the ocean water begin in our **atmosphere**, which is formed by gases that surround Earth. Storms happen because the atmosphere is always moving. The hotter air is lighter and rises. Cooler air flows in to take its place. This constant movement creates winds.

When winds blows on the surface of the ocean, waves form. The blowing winds can also create ocean currents. Currents are like rivers of cold and warm water that flow within the ocean itself. Warm currents travel away from the equator while cool ones flow back toward it. The equator is an imaginary line that runs around the middle of Earth. It is always hot near the equator.

Pacific

equator

Indian

I am especially interested in the way ocean animals behave and wanted to observe some that had come close to shore.

Do they do this when a storm is near? I wanted to see if this was true.

8

Ocean animals

A humpback whale dives in the warm waters of the Pacific Ocean.

Some sea life behave in a special way in stormy weather.

Severe storms can affect a whale's ability to use its sonar, a way of detecting objects using sound. When whales make a noise, they send sound waves into the area around them. The sound waves bounce off objects and return to the whale. This allows them to locate objects and sense their shape and movement.

Storm petrels are small sea birds that can be found in all of the world's oceans. They spend most of their time hovering above the water. They soar by gliding across the tops of the waves, gaining energy from the wind.

The storm petrel gets it name due to the fact that it avoids land except during very stormy weather or at night. Their small, thin legs can only hold their weight for a few steps, which is why they prefer to fly over the ocean waters.

Storm petrels soar over the Atlantic Ocean.

A humpback breaches to take in air.

So now you know why I was
out in a boat when the storm came.
I discovered that young sharks that usually
swim in shallow water, swim out to deeper
water when they sense a storm is coming.
It seems they can sense even the smallest
change in **air pressure**.

A shark's ears have small hairs that move
when a change in air pressure is detected.
This movement sends a message to the
shark's brain making the shark change
its behavior.

Air pressure is the weight of the air and how hard it is pressing down on Earth. Low pressure affects the weather. Air rises in areas of low pressure. The rising air holds water vapor, which cools, forms clouds, and falls as rain.

Some scientists think we could get advance warning of bad storms by watching sharks.

The huge waves came out of nowhere. The storm had started far out to sea. I was taken by surprise!

The heaviest rain and strongest winds occur right next to the eye of the hurricane.

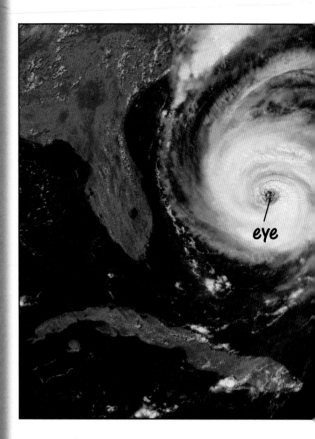

eye

The coastline is battered by winds and waves.

Where hurricanes come from

A **hurricane**, also called a tropical cyclone, is a low-pressure area with powerful winds and thunderstorms. It rotates in the atmosphere over water. Hurricanes begin near the equator, in warm, tropical waters. Heat from the sun causes warm, moist air to rise over the water. The rising air creates a ring of low pressure called an eye, and winds begin to rotate around it.

At first, the eye can be hundreds of miles across, so the winds are not strong. But as it narrows, the winds gain speed. At their fastest, the winds are traveling at 186 miles per hour (300 kph).

Huge trees can be uprooted in a powerful hurricane.

As the hurricane spins, it takes in huge amounts of water vapor. The winds rise and cool, the vapor condenses into water droplets, and the droplets fall in torrential rain.

The storm passed over as quickly as it had come. I spotted a waterspout moving away in the distance. That had to be what had tossed me around.

My small boat had been picked up and carried out to sea. I was now a long way from the shoreline. It would take me a long time to row back. By now, the water was choppy with waves.

Waterspouts

A waterspout is a funnel-shaped spiral of air that develops over water. The spout is connected to a cloud above. Waterspouts don't suck up water. Clouds of water vapor inside the funnel provide the water. The water in the funnel is formed when the water vapor cools and becomes a liquid.

Most waterspouts move fairly slowly and last between five to ten minutes, although some can last up to an hour. Much stronger ones may happen after a severe thunderstorm.

Luckily, I could do some science research with the equipment I had on board. I got out my wave monitor, which measures the size and movement of waves while it bobs on the surface of the sea.

It's useful in predicting changes in the way waves behave. This instrument can tell when a heavy storm is coming.

A wave is ready to break, or curl.

Waves follow one another into shore.

Water tumbles over as a wave breaks.

How waves are made

Most waves are made by the wind. The stronger and longer the wind blows in one direction, the bigger the wave becomes.

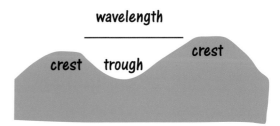

The distance between the crests, or tops, of waves is called the **wavelength**.

When the wind passes over the surface of the ocean, it pulls at the water and causes the surface to move. The water close to the surface turns over in a circular movement, forming a rounded shape as it spins. Below the surface, the circles of water sink deeper and deeper and dissolve.

Close to the beach, the circling movement slows. The top part of the circle flows over the top and the wave breaks.

movement of wind

spinning water particles

Salty sea

If you've ever swallowed seawater, you know it tastes salty. That's because of the salt, or **sodium chloride**, in the water of the world's oceans. It comes from rocks and soil on land. For millions of years, salt has been washed into the oceans by rivers through **erosion**.

Not all oceans have the same amount of salt. Some are saltier than others. Deep below the surface, currents are driven by saltiness and temperature changes. Changes in salt amounts affect the water's **density**, or how tightly packed its molecules are. This can contribute to changes in currents, affecting weather.

This satellite picture shows salty areas in red and less salty areas in dark blue and purple.

The Dead Sea is a lake that lies between Israel and Jordan. It contains the saltiest water on Earth. It's nine times saltier than seawater. This area is extremely hot and water evaporates quickly leaving behind salt minerals that mix with the remaining water. This causes the lake to become more and more salty.

Salt water is denser than the human body, so it's easy to float in the Dead Sea.

Salt deposits pile up along the shore of the Dead Sea.

My little boat may have been
small, but it was sturdy and
stayed afloat. I needed to
get back to shore,
so I grabbed the oars
and started to row.

Floating ships

You might wonder how a ship made of heavy steel can float. If you threw a chunk of steel into a pond, it would certainly sink to the bottom.

It sinks because steel has a greater density than water. Density is a measure of how tightly packed together the material in something is.

A ship may be made of steel, but there's more than just steel inside it. Air fills the empty space inside a ship or a rowboat. Air is less dense than water. Together, the steel of the ship's frame and the air inside the ship have less density than water, so the ship floats.

The storm had driven me way off course and the coast ahead looked rocky and dangerous. I knew that ships had been shipwrecked on these shores and landing my small boat might be difficult.

I put my underwater robot to work. Tiny robots like this one are great for doing scientific research at the bottom of the ocean. They can also find wrecks—even sunken treasure!

Shipwreck!

Sometimes severe storms can cause shipwrecks. When sailing ships crossed the oceans centuries ago, they were not as safe as today's modern steel ships. A sailing ship could be driven onto a rocky coastline in a storm and end up shattered on the rocks.

Today, ocean explorers use robots to inspect underwater pipelines, search for treasure, and explore wrecks.

More than a thousand wrecks lie scattered off the Skeleton Coast, in Namibia, Africa.

By now the storm was rising again and I needed to get to land. I could see a **lighthouse** on the cliffs ahead and a small cove to the left. Maybe I could row toward that small, protected inlet and land the boat safely.

24

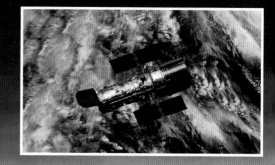

Satellites monitor storm activity from space and send photographs of cloud formations back to Earth.

Watching storms

Storms can cause terrible damage on land and are also dangerous at sea. Monitoring storms is an important scientific activity.

Satellites, weather balloons, and aircraft make up a worldwide network that gathers information.

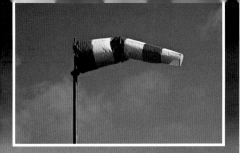

A wind sock indicates which direction the wind is blowing.

An anemometer uses spinning cups to measure wind speed.

Some aircraft, like this WC-130J Hercules, can fly right into a hurricane and out the other side.

Also, thousands of **weather stations** set up on the ground around the world provide data and send information back each day. The stations contain instruments such as barometers to measure air pressure, rain gauges, and wind socks. A hygrometer measures humidity, which is the amount of water vapor in the air.

Special aircraft with instruments fly into storm clouds, and even hurricanes. They measure temperature, pressure, and wind movement. The wings and body of the aircraft are reinforced so they can stand up to the forces they fly through and hold up under the weight of ice that may form on them.

But now the waves were lashing the rocks and my boat was being tossed around like a small cork. I couldn't use the oars any longer.

I waited for the waves to carry me where they would...

And, just as they threatened to turn over the boat and me with it, I saw the rescue boat approaching. They had seen me struggling and were coming to save me. Relieved, I climbed into their boat, and they towed my boat behind us.

Lighthouses

A lighthouse is a tower with a large, bright light at the top. Lighthouses are built on coasts to guide ships safely toward a harbor or warn them of dangerous rocks.

The most important part of a lighthouse is the light. It is designed to be visible over long distances and through bad weather.

Sailors know which lighthouse they are looking at by the characteristics of the light. Each lighthouse light flashes at a set rate and for a certain amount of time. All ships have a list of these characteristics so they can identify each lighthouse.

Rescue boats go out in stormy seas to help boats and ships in trouble.

They brought me and my boat to shore. I was safe and so was my equipment.

It had been an adventure. Still, I had collected useful information. I'd observed sharks, used my wave monitor, and best of all, put my treasure-seeking robot to good work!

Warming oceans

Scientists believe that the oceans of the world are growing warmer. They believe heat-trapping gases in the atmosphere are increasing and holding in more heat than ever. The gradual warming of Earth's atmosphere due to these gases is called **global warming.**

The oceans are absorbing most of the extra heat. More than 90% of the extra heat generated over the last 50 years has gone into the oceans. Most of the heat is gathered in the upper layers of the oceans, but warming has been observed in the deeper regions as well.

Where does global warming go?

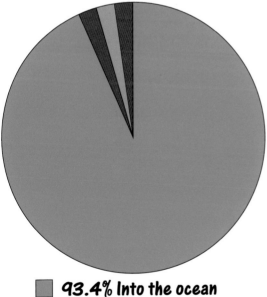

93.4% Into the ocean
2.3% Into the atmosphere
2.2% Into the land
2.1% Into the Arctic

Warmer oceans may not seem that important, but they can cause huge problems. Melting ice caps have raised sea levels around the world. Temperature changes in the oceans affect the weather. The weather patterns change as a result, creating stronger storms and more floods.

Changing weather patterns can cause flooding in places that do not normally experience floods.

Glossary

air pressure
A measure of how hard the air presses down on Earth's surface

atmosphere
A combination of gases that extends from Earth into space and is identified by layers

breaches
Leaps out of the water; used especially with whales

density
The amount of matter in a set space of a material and how closely packed its molecules are

erosion
The moving of rocks and soil caused by weathering. Water, wind, and ice carry away the weathered material

evaporates
Changes from a liquid, such as water, to a vapor or mist

global warming
The gradual increase of the temperature in Earth's atmosphere from heat-trapping gases released by the burning of fossil fuels

hurricane
A severe tropical storm that develops around an area of low pressure and blows extremely strong winds around a center point called the eye

lighthouse
A tall, fixed structure with a bright light at the top used to guide ships and warn of hazards along the coastline

sodium chloride
The name for the chemical formula of salt, which is a white, cube-shaped crystal

sonar
A system which uses echoes or reflected sound waves to detect objects underwater or to measure the depth of the sea floor. An instrument or an animal sends out pulses of sound which bounce back when they hit a solid object.

wavelength
The measure of the distance between the crest, or top, of one wave to the crest of the following wave

weather stations
Places that hold equipment for measuring rainfall, wind speed, temperature, and other data in order to monitor and predict a region's weather

Learn More...

Books:

Superstorm Sandy
by Lynn Peppas.
Crabtree Publishing, 2014.

How to Survive Being Lost at Sea (Prepare to Survive)
by Tim O'Shei.
Edge Books, 2009.

Global Warming Alert!
by Dr. Richard Cheel.
Crabtree Publishing, 2007.

Websites:

These interesting websites provide more fascinating ocean facts:
www.mbgnet.net/salt/oceans/index.htm
http://school.discoveryeducation.com/schooladventures/planetocean/
http://legacy.mos.org/oceans/planet/index.html

Find out how divers communicate with each other underwater using hand signals.
www.seagrant.wisc.edu/madisonjason11/diving_signals.html

Find out the facts about hurricanes.
www.sciencekids.co.nz/sciencefacts/weather/hurricane.html

Index